Scholastic Success With Writing
Grade 2

by Lisa Molengraft

SCHOLASTIC
PROFESSIONAL BOOKS

New York • Toronto • London • Auckland • Sydney •
Mexico City • New Delhi • Hong Kong • Buenos Aires

Scholastic Inc. grants teachers permission to photocopy the reproducible pages from this book for classroom use. No other part of this publication may be reproduced in whole or in part, or stored in a retrieval system, or transmitted in any form or by any means, electronic, mechanical, photocopying, recording, or otherwise without written permission of the publisher. For information regarding permission, write to Scholastic Inc., 557 Broadway, New York, NY 10012.

Cover art by Victoria Raymond
Cover design by Maria Lilja
Interior illustrations by Mark Mason
Interior design by Quack & Company

ISBN 0-439-44495-0

Copyright © 2002 Scholastic, Inc.
All rights reserved. Printed in the U.S.A.

1 2 3 4 5 6 7 8 9 10   40   09 08 07 06 05 04 03

Introduction

One of the greatest challenges teachers and parents face is helping children develop independent writing skills. Each writing experience is unique and individualized, making it each child's responsibility to plan, expand, and proofread his or her work. However, the high-interest topics and engaging exercises in this book will both stimulate and encourage children as they develop the necessary skills to become independent writers. This book uses these strategies to introduce grade-appropriate skills that can be used in daily writing assignments such as journals, stories, and letters. Like a stepladder, this book will help children reach the next level of independent writing.

Table of Contents

You're Sharp! *(Capitalizing sentence beginnings)* 4
Stick With It *(Capitalizing sentence beginnings)* 5
A Whale of a Sentence *(Punctuating statements)* 6
That Sounds Fishy to Me *(Writing statements)* 7
Ask Mother Goose *(Punctuating questions)* 8
Ask the Wolf *(Writing questions)* 9
Is Your Head in the Clouds? *(Punctuating statements and questions)* 10
Sunny Sentences *(Capitalizing/punctuating statements and questions)* 11
Camp Fiddlestick *(Writing statements and questions)* 12
A Happy Camper *(Proofreading statements and questions)* 13
A Day at the Beach *(Punctuating exclamations)* 14
Seashore Sentences *(Writing statements, questions, and exclamations)* 15
Building Blocks *(Building sentences)* 16
Keep Building! *(Building sentences)* 17
Get Your Ticket! *(Building sentences)* 18
Slide Show *(Building sentences)* 19
Mystery Bags *(Brainstorming descriptive words)* 20
Country Roads *(Writing descriptive words)* 21
It's in the Bag *(Adding descriptive words)* 22
City Streets *(Writing descriptive sentences)* 23
Football Frenzy *(Expanding sentences)* 24
Take Me Out to the Ball Game *(Expanding sentences)* 25

Cake and Ice Cream *(Combining sentences)* 26
Salt and Pepper *(Combining sentences)* 27
Great Gardening Tips *(Combining sentences)* 28
Growing Sentences *(Combining sentences)* 29
The Sky's the Limit *(Using commas in a series)* ... 30
Up, Up, and Away *(Using commas in a series)* 31
Out of This World *(Proofreading)* 32
Smart About Saturn *(Proofreading)* 33
Banana-Rama *(Choosing the correct verb)* 34
An Apple a Day *(Choosing the correct verb)* 35
Stories of Nature *(Completing a sequenced story)* 36
Nestled in a Nest *(Writing a sequenced story)* 37
Stories on Parade *(Writing the middle and end of stories)* 38
An Original Story *(Writing the beginning, middle, and end of a story)* 39
Once Upon a Time *(Mapping a story: The setting)* 40
All Kinds of Characters *(Mapping a story: The characters)* 41
That's a Problem! *(Mapping a story: The problem)* 42
Good Solution! *(Mapping a story: The solution)* 43
The Mighty Knight *(Writing a story from a map)* 44
A Story Fit for a King *(Mapping and writing a story)* 45
The Father of Our Country *(Proofreading)* 46
Presidential Pen Pals *(Writing a friendly letter)* ... 47
Answer Key 48

Name _____

Capitalizing sentence beginnings

You're Sharp!

 A sentence begins with a capital letter.

Circle the words that show the correct way to begin each sentence.

- many Of / Many of — my friends are in second grade.
- Our teacher / our Teacher — keeps a fish tank in our classroom.
- The reading / the reading — center has many good books.
- the globe / The globe — helps us find places around the world.
- we Study / We study — about the weather.
- Our class / our Class — won the reading contest.

Name _____

Capitalizing sentence beginnings

Stick With It

 A sentence begins with a capital letter.

Write the beginning words correctly to make a sentence.

1. art class _____ begins at noon.

2. today we _____ are making clay pots.

3. first, we _____ form the clay into balls.

4. the next _____ step is to make a hole in the ball.

5. my teacher _____ dries the pots.

6. next week _____ we will paint the pots.

Scholastic Success With Writing • 5

Name _____ Punctuating statements

A Whale of a Sentence

➡ A **telling sentence** ends with a **period** (.).

Rewrite the sentences using capital letters and periods.

1. the blue whale is the largest animal in the world
   _____

2. even dinosaurs were not as large as the blue whale
   _____

3. blue whales are not part of the fish family
   _____

4. the blue whale has no teeth
   _____

5. blue whales eat tiny sea creatures
   _____

6. blue whales have two blowholes
   _____

Name _____

Writing statements

That Sounds Fishy to Me

➡ *A* **telling sentence** *begins with a* **capital letter** *and ends with a* **period**.

Write a sentence about each fish. Remember to tell a complete idea.

1. The swordfish has a long snout _____
2. _____
3. _____
4. _____
5. _____
6. _____
7. _____

Scholastic Success With Writing • Grade 2

Name _____

Punctuating questions

Ask Mother Goose

 A sentence that asks a question ends with a **question mark (?)**. It often begins with one of these words.

Who . . .   Where . . .   Why . . .   Could . . .
What . . .   When . . .   Will . . .

Rewrite the questions using capital letters and question marks.

1. where is the king's castle

_____

2. who helped Humpty Dumpty

_____

3. why did the cow jump over the moon

_____

4. will the frog become a prince

_____

5. could the three mice see

_____

8   Scholastic Success With Writing • Grade 2

Name _____   **Writing questions**

Ask the Wolf

An **asking sentence** begins with a **capital letter** and ends with a **question mark (?)**. It often begins with one of these words.

How . . .   Can . . .   Would . . .
Did . . .   Is . . .   Should . . .

Imagine that you can meet the Big Bad Wolf. What questions would you ask him about Little Red Riding Hood and the Three Little Pigs? Use a different beginning word for each question you write.

1. How _____
2. Did _____
3. Can _____

1. Is _____
2. Should _____
3. Would _____

 Pretend that you are the Big Bad Wolf. Write a sentence on another piece of paper to answer each question above.

Scholastic Success With Writing • Grade 2   9

Name _____

Punctuating statements and questions

Is Your Head in the Clouds?

 A **telling sentence** *ends with a* **period** *(.).*
An **asking sentence** *ends with a* **question mark** *(?).*

Finish each sentence by putting a period or a question mark in the cloud at the end.

1. Clouds can look like cotton balls, feathers, or blankets ◯

2. Do you know what makes a cloud form in the sky ◯

3. Have you ever seen dark clouds on rainy days ◯

4. Dark clouds may bring thunderstorms ◯

5. Can you imagine pictures in the clouds ◯

6. White clouds drift across the blue sky ◯

7. Why don't we see clouds every day ◯

8. Rain, snow, sleet, and hail may fall from clouds ◯

 Find two telling sentences and two questions in one of your favorite books. Write them on another piece of paper.

Name _____

Capitalizing/punctuating statements and questions

Sunny

Every sentence begins with a capital letter.
A telling sentence ends with a period (.).
An asking sentence ends with a question mark (?).

Rewrite each sentence correctly.

1. the sun is the closest star to Earth

   _____

2. the sun is not the brightest star

   _____

3. what is the temperature of the sun

   _____

4. the sun is a ball of hot gas

   _____

5. how large is the sun

   _____

6. will the sun ever burn out

   _____

 On another piece of paper, write a sentence with two mistakes. Ask a friend to circle the mistakes.

Name _____

Writing statements and questions

Camp Fiddlestick

 A telling sentence is called a **statement**. *An asking sentence is called a* **question**. *Now ask yourself:*

How do sentences begin? How do statements end? How do questions end?

Write three statements and three questions about the picture.

Statements:

1. _____

2. _____

3. _____

Questions:

1. _____

2. _____

3. _____

 Sing "Where is Thumbkin?" to yourself. Count the number of questions and statements in the song.

Name _____

Proofreading statements and questions

A Happy Camper

➡ *Complete:*
Every sentence begins with a _____.
A statement ends with a _____.
A question ends with a _____.

Uh oh! Dalton was in a hurry when he wrote this letter. Help him find 10 mistakes. Circle them.

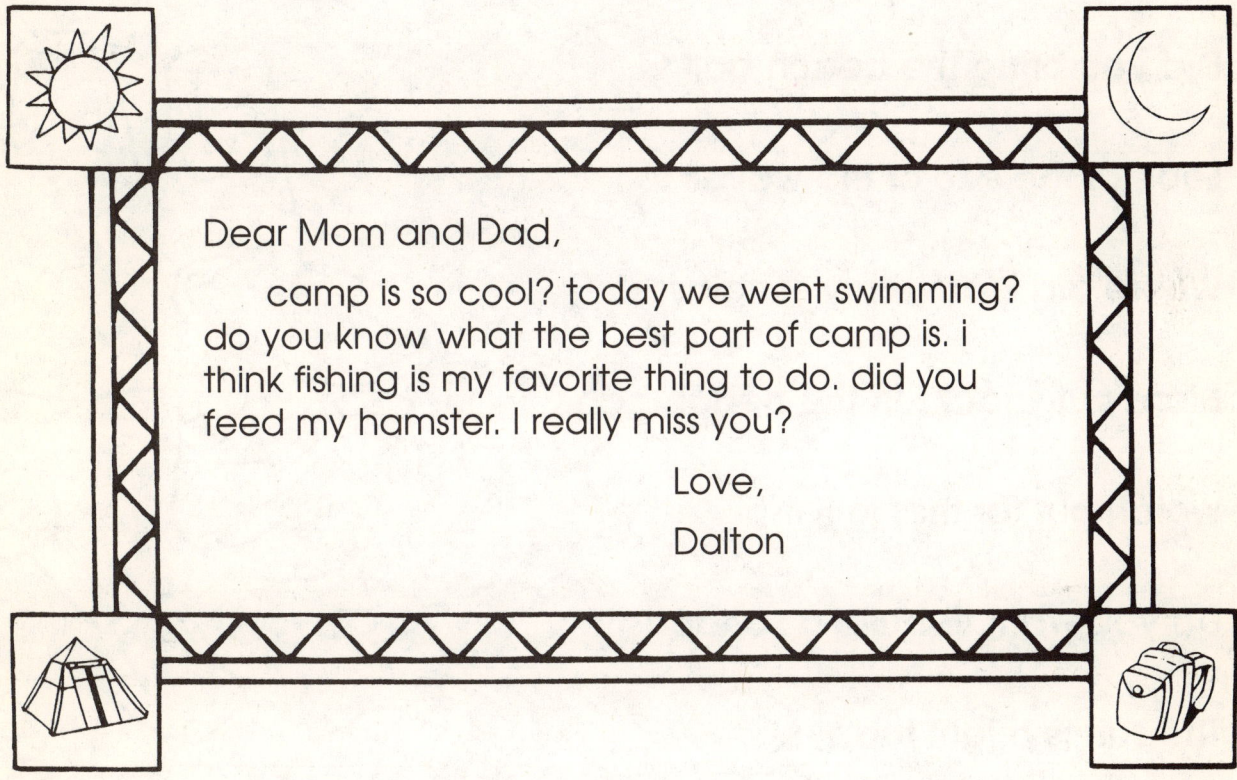

Dear Mom and Dad,

  camp is so cool? today we went swimming? do you know what the best part of camp is. i think fishing is my favorite thing to do. did you feed my hamster. I really miss you?

  Love,

  Dalton

Now choose two questions and two statements from Dalton's letter. Rewrite each correctly.

1. _____

2. _____

3. _____

4. _____

 On another piece of paper, write a letter to a friend or family member. Include two statements and two questions.

Scholastic Success With Writing • Grade 2   13

Name _____

Punctuating exclamations

A Day at the Beach

 A sentence that shows strong feeling or excitement is called an **exclamation**. It ends with an **exclamation point** (!). For example: Look at that shark!

Finish each sentence by putting a period, a question mark, or an exclamation point in the shell at the end.

1. I wonder if Jamie will be at the beach today ◠
2. Did you bring the beach ball ◠
3. Look at the size of the waves ◠
4. Where did I leave my sunglasses ◠
5. Mom put snacks in the beach bag ◠
6. Watch out for that jellyfish ◠
7. Do you want to build a sandcastle ◠
8. The sun is bright today ◠
9. Did you see that sailboat ◠
10. Don't step on that starfish ◠
11. It is windy near the seashore ◠
12. Should we put up an umbrella ◠

 Read these sentences: I see a sand crab. I see a sand crab! How does your voice change?

14 Scholastic Success With Writing • Grade 2

Name _____

Writing statements, questions, and exclamations

Seashore Sentences

➡ *Complete:*
A _____ ends with a period.
A _____ ends with a question mark.
An _____ ends with an exclamation point.

Write a statement (S), a question (Q), and an exclamation (E) about each picture.

S _____
_____

Q _____
_____

E _____
_____

S _____
_____

Q _____
_____

E _____
_____

 On another piece of paper, write a statement, a question, and an exclamation about a cartoon in the newspaper.

Scholastic Success With Writing • Grade 2   15

Name _____   Building sentences

Building Blocks

 A good sentence has a part that tells who or what the sentence is about. This is called the **subject**.

Make a list of possible subjects to complete each sentence.

_____ jumped the fence.
1. _____
2. _____
3. _____

_____ is too full.
1. _____
2. _____
3. _____

 A good sentence has a part that tells what happens. This is called the **action**.

Make a list of possible actions to complete each sentence.

We _____ on the playground.
1. _____
2. _____
3. _____

The cowboy _____ on his horse.
1. _____
2. _____
3. _____

 On another piece of paper, make a list of five subjects you would like to write about.

Name _____ Building sentences

Keep Building!

 Some sentences have a part that tells where or when the action is happening.

For each sentence, make a list of possible endings that tell where or when the action happens.

The wind blew _____.
1. _____
2. _____
3. _____

The baby tripped _____.
1. _____
2. _____
3. _____

Complete each sentence.

1. _____ made us laugh last night.

2. The door leads _____.

3. The crowd _____ at the circus.

4. The paint bucket spilled _____.

5. _____ was never seen again.

6. The firefighter _____ into the fire truck.

Name _____   **Building sentences**

Get Your Ticket!

Write a sentence to match each picture. Be sure to include a subject, an action, and a part that tells where or when.

1. A boy climbs a tree in his backyard.

2. _____

3. _____

 Find a cartoon in the newspaper. Use the pictures to write a sentence on another piece of paper. Be sure to include a subject, an action, and a part that tells where or when.

Name _____   **Building sentences**

Slide Show

 A sentence is more interesting when it includes a subject, an action, and a part that tells where or when.

Write three sentences and draw pictures to match.

subject	action	where or when

1. _____

subject	action	where or when

2. _____

subject	action	where or when

3. _____

 Switch the sentence parts around to make three silly sentences! Write the sentences on another piece of paper.

Scholastic Success With Writing • Grade 2

Name _____

Brainstorming descriptive words

Mystery Bags

 Describing words help you imagine how something looks, feels, smells, sounds, or tastes.

Make a list of words that describe the object in each bag below.

 Use a paper sack to make a real mystery bag. Place an object in the bag and give describing clues to someone at home. Can he or she guess the mystery object?

20 Scholastic SUCCESS With Writing • Grade 2

Name _____ Writing descriptive words

Country Roads

 A good sentence uses describing words to help the reader "paint a picture" in his or her mind.

Add a describing word from the list to finish each sentence.

1. The _____ chicken laid _____ eggs in her nest.

2. The _____ barn keeps the _____ animals warm at night.

3. _____ carrots grow in the _____ garden.

4. Two _____ pigs sleep in the _____ pen.

5. The _____ cows drink from the _____ pond.

6. A _____ scarecrow frightens the _____ birds.

wooden
sunny
lazy
black
three
orange
thirsty
cold
shallow
muddy
funny
fat

 On another piece of paper, write three sentences describing your favorite place to visit.

Name _____   Adding descriptive words

It's in the Bag

 Describing words *make a sentence more interesting.*

Add a describing word to each sentence.

1. My friend's _____ dog has fleas!

2. The _____ popcorn is in the big bowl.

3. How did the _____ worm get on the sidewalk?

4. The _____ ocean waves crashed against the rocks.

5. The _____ ball broke a window at school!

6. My _____ skin itched from poison ivy.

7. The two _____ squirrels chased each other up the tree.

8. The _____ sand felt good on my feet.

9. Are the _____ apples ready to be picked?

10. The _____ ball was hard to catch.

11. Is the _____ salamander hiding under the rock?

12. The _____ snow cone melted quickly.

 Ask someone at home to make a mystery bag and give you clues about the object inside.

22   Scholastic Success With Writing • Grade 2

Name _____

Writing descriptive sentences

City Streets

 A good sentence uses describing words.

Write a statement (S), a question (Q), and an exclamation (E) about the picture. Use each of the following describing words:

fast **busy** **crowded**

S _____
_____

Q _____
_____

E _____
_____

 Describe a "mystery object" to a friend. Can he or she guess what you are describing?

Scholastic Success With Writing • Grade 2 23

Name _____   Expanding sentences

Football Frenzy

 A sentence is more interesting when it gives exact information.

Replace each word to make the sentence more exact.

1. The ⟨ball⟩ game starts ⟨soon⟩.

   The ___soccer___ game starts ___now___.

2. We are meeting ⟨her⟩ ⟨there⟩.

   We are meeting _____ _____.

3. Let's eat ⟨this⟩ and ⟨that⟩ before the game.

   Let's eat _____ and _____ before the game.

4. I hope ⟨they⟩ score ⟨some⟩ points.

   I hope _____ score _____ points.

5. ⟨They⟩ were also ⟨there⟩.

   _____ were also _____.

6. ⟨He⟩ played a ⟨good⟩ game!

   _____ played a _____ game!

Name _____

Expanding sentences

Take Me Out to the Ball Game

 A sentence is more interesting when it gives complete information.

Finish each sentence so that it answers the (question.)

1. The players get to the stadium (when.)

   _____

2. The team is excited because (why.)

   _____

3. The fans arrive in (what.)

   _____

4. Flags are flying (where.)

   _____

5. A man sings the "Star-Spangled Banner" (when.)

   _____

6. The fans cheer for (whom.)

   _____

7. The ball is hit (where.)

   _____

 On another piece of paper, write a sentence about your favorite game. Be sure to tell who plays the game with you.

Scholastic Success With Writing • Grade 2   25

Name _____

Combining sentences

Cake and Ice Cream

 Two sentences that share the same subject can be combined to make one sentence by using the word and.

Rewrite the sentences by combining their endings.

1. The party was fun.
   The party was exciting.

2. We blew up orange balloons.
   We blew up red balloons.

   _____

3. We ate cake.
   We ate ice cream.

   _____

4. The cake frosting was green.
   The cake frosting was yellow.

   _____

5. We made a bookmark.
   We made a clay pot.

   _____

6. We brought games.
   We brought prizes.

   _____

26   Scholastic Success With Writing • Grade 2

Name _____   **Combining sentences**

Salt and Pepper

 Two sentences that share the same ending can also be combined to make one sentence.

Rewrite the sentences by combining their subjects.

1. These peanuts are salty!
   These pretzels are salty!

   <u>These peanuts and pretzels are salty!</u>

2. The first graders eat lunch at noon.
   The second graders eat lunch at noon.

   _____

3. Where is the salt?
   Where is the pepper?

   _____

4. The napkins are on the table.
   The forks are on the table.

   _____

5. Are the muffins in the oven?
   Are the cookies in the oven?

   _____

6. Michael bought lunch today.
   Stephen bought lunch today.

   _____

Scholastic Success With Writing • Grade 2

Name _____ **Combining sentences**

Great Gardening Tips

 Sentences can also be combined to make them more interesting. Key words can help put two sentences together.

I will plan my garden. I am waiting for spring.

I will plan my garden while I am waiting for spring.

Combine the two sentences using the key word. Write a new sentence.

1. **Fill a cup with water. Add some flower seeds.**

_____

2. **This will soften the seeds. They are hard.**

_____

3. **Fill a cup with dirt. The seeds soak in water.**

_____

4. **Bury the seeds in the cup. The dirt covers them.**

_____

5. **Add water to the plant. Do not add too much.**

_____

6. **Set the cup in the sun. The plant will grow.**

_____

Name _____   **Combining sentences**

Growing Sentences

 Sentences can be combined to make them more interesting.

Write a combined sentence of your own. Use the given key word to help you.

1. while I watch TV while my mom makes lunch.

2. until _____

3. because _____

4. but _____

5. or _____

6. and _____

 On another piece of paper, write a combined sentence of your own using one of these key words: *after, before, during.*

Scholastic Success With Writing • Grade 2

Name _____   Using commas in a series

The Sky's the Limit

 Some sentences include a list. A **comma** (,) is used to separate each item in the list.

For example: Mrs. Jones asked the class to work on pages two, three, and four.

Fill in the blanks to make a list in each sentence. Watch for commas!

1. I ate _____, _____, and _____ for breakfast.

2. We stayed with Grandma on _____, _____, and _____ nights.

3. I found _____, _____, and _____ in my party bag.

4. The boys played _____, _____, and _____ at summer camp.

5. The _____, _____, and _____ ate the corn we scattered.

6. The pigs built their houses using _____, _____, and _____.

 Cut a balloon out of paper. On one side, list three objects that fly. On the other side, write a sentence that lists these objects.

30   Scholastic Success With Writing • Grade 2

Name _____   Using commas in a series

Up, Up, and Away

 *Some sentences include a list. A **comma** (,) is used to separate each item in the list.*

Write a sentence that includes a list of the words that are given.

**coat
hat
gloves**

1. _____
_____

2. _____
_____

**spelling
reading
math**

**bread
peanut butter
jelly**

3. _____
_____

4. _____
_____

**birds
flowers
butterflies**

 On another piece of paper, write a sentence that lists colors or shapes of balloons.

Scholastic Success With Writing • Grade 2   31

Name _____   Proofreading

Out of This World

After you write a sentence, go back and look for mistakes. This is called **proofreading** your work.

Use the proofreading marks to correct the two mistakes in each sentence.

<u>mars</u> = Make a capital letter.   ? = Add a question mark.   ! = Add an exclamation point.

. = Add a period.   , = Add a comma.   ☐ = Add a word. (Write a describing word in the box.)

1. Sometimes I can see mars Jupiter, and Saturn with my telescope.

2. There are ☐ ∧ stars in our galaxy

3. comets are ☐ ∧ pieces of ice and rock.

4. The sun is really a ☐ ∧ star

5. is there life on any other planet

6. Look at that ☐ ∧ shooting star

7. can you imagine traveling in space

8. i think I saw a ☐ ∧ alien.

💡 On another piece of paper, write two sentences about space with two mistakes in each. Ask someone at home to proofread your sentences. Is he or she correct?

32   Scholastic Success With Writing • Grade 2

Name _____   **Proofreading**

Smart About Saturn

 Be sure to proofread your work.

Matthew's science report has nine mistakes. Use proofreading marks to correct his work. Then rewrite the report. Add at least two describing words to the report.

**Saturn
by Matthew**

Saturn is famous for the rings that surround it? its rings are made of ice, rock and dirt. The rings circle around the planet! Saturn is made of gas? saturn's gases are lighter than water That means Saturn would float if you put it into a tub of water Saturn has at least 17 moons

_____
_____
_____
_____
_____

 On another piece of paper, write a short report about your favorite planet. Be sure to proofread it when you are done.

Scholastic Success With Writing • Grade 2   33

Name _____

Choosing the correct verb

Banana-Rama

Color the word that is missing from each sentence.

1. We _____ a spelling test yesterday. taked / took
2. There _____ frost on the ground. was / were
3. Tommy _____ the Statue of Liberty. seen / saw
4. How _____ elephants are at the zoo? much / many
5. Claire _____ her lizard to school. brought / brang
6. Have you _____ my dog? seen / saw
7. Alyssa _____ a new pair of skates. gots / has
8. You _____ supposed to finish your work. are / is
9. We _____ standing near a snake! were / was
10. They _____ a pig in the mud. seen / saw
11. We _____ our winter boots. wore / weared
12. Is she _____ to come over? gonna / going
13. _____ your cat climb trees? Do / Does
14. Rosie _____ cookies to the bake sale. brang / brought

Name _____

Choosing the correct verb

An Apple a Day

Find the word that is incorrect in each sentence. Draw an apple around it and write the correct word on the line.

1. Laura brang a snack to camp. _____

2. I seen the sea lion show at the zoo. _____

3. Drew gots a dinosaur collection. _____

4. Mara taked her dog for a walk. _____

5. We is going to see the movie. _____

6. Jason runned to the playground. _____

7. How many pennies do you got? _____

8. The kids was having fun. _____

9. Did you saw the soccer game? _____

10. How much do that cost? _____

11. Kelly brang her cat to school! _____

12. I does my homework after school. _____

 Eat an apple. Then on another piece of paper, write a statement, a question, and an exclamation describing the apple. Be sure each sentence uses correct words.

Stories of Nature

 Sentences should be written in the correct order to tell a story.

Finish the stories by writing a sentence about each of the last two pictures.

First: Two birds build a nest.

Next: _____

Last: _____

First: A flower bud grows.

Next: _____

Last: _____

Name _____ **Writing a sequenced story**

Nestled in a Nest

Write a sentence about each picture to make your own story.

 Read your story to a friend.

Name _____

Writing the middle and end of stories

Stories on Parade

➡ Stories have a **beginning** (B), a **middle** (M), and an **end** (E).

Write a middle sentence that tells what happens next. Then write an ending sentence that tells what happens last.

B During the parade, five funny clowns jumped out of a purple bus.

M Next, _____

E Last, _____

B A big balloon got loose in the wind.

M Next, _____

E Last, _____

B A group of horses stopped right in front of us.

M Next, _____

E Last, _____

B Some clowns were riding motorcycles.

M Next, _____

E Last, _____

 On another piece of paper, draw a picture of a parade that shows what is happening in the stories you wrote.

Name _____

Writing the beginning, middle, and end of a story

An Original Story

Choose a story idea from the list. Then write a beginning, middle, and ending sentence to make a story of your own. Color a picture to match each part.

- The Best Birthday Ever
- My Dog's Dream
- King for a Day
- The Magic Rock

First: _____
_____
_____
_____

Next: _____
_____
_____
_____

Last: _____
_____
_____
_____

 Staple three pieces of paper together to make a book. Write another story and draw a picture for each part.

Scholastic Success With Writing • Grade 2

Name _____ Mapping a story:
The setting

Once Upon a Time

 The **setting** of a story tells when or where it is happening.

Imagine that you are writing a story for each picture below. How will you describe the setting? Write a sentence describing each setting.

setting → characters → problem → solution

 It was a hot morning in the desert.

 On another piece of paper, describe the setting of your favorite movie.

Name _____

**Mapping a story:
The characters**

All Kinds of Characters

 The people or animals in a story are called **characters**.

Some characters are likable and others are not. Write a describing sentence about each character. Be sure to give each character a name.

setting → characters → problem → solution

_____
_____
_____

_____
_____
_____

_____
_____
_____

 On another piece of paper, make a list of four people you know well. Write three words that describe each of them. Cross out the four names and write animal names instead. Now you have four characters to use in your next story!

Name _____

Mapping a story:
The problem

That's a Problem!

 To make a story exciting, one of the characters often runs into a **problem**.

Think about each character in the sentences below. What could happen that would make a problem for that character? Write the next sentence creating a problem.

setting → characters → **problem** → solution

1. Beauty Butterfly was enjoying the warm spring day.

_____

2. Jesse was supposed to wear shoes outside.

_____

3. Gabby could not wait to bite into her apple.

_____

4. Ben smacked the baseball into the air.

_____

5. Barney Bass had never seen such a big worm!

_____

Name _____

Mapping a story:
The solution

Good Solution!

➡ *At the end of a story, the problem is usually solved. This is called the **solution**.*
Read the beginning and middle parts of the stories below. Write an ending solution for each.

| setting | → | characters | → | problem | → | **solution** |

David and his dog, Spot, were best friends. They went everywhere together. At bedtime, David whistled for Spot to jump in his bed. One winter night, David whistled and whistled, but Spot did not come.

_____

_____

_____

Josh loved second grade, but he did not like recess. Josh's class was always the last one out to the playground. Every day, Josh ran to get a swing, but they were always taken.

_____

_____

_____

 On another piece of paper, make a list of three problems you have faced. How did you solve each problem?

Scholastic Success With Writing • Grade 2   43

Name _____

Writing a story from a map

The Mighty Knight

 A **story map** helps you plan the setting, characters, problem, and solution.

Write a sentence about each part of the map to make a story.

_____

 Read your story to a friend.

44 Scholastic Success With Writing • Grade 2

Name _____

Mapping and writing a story

A Story Fit for a King

 Use a story map to help plan your story before you begin writing.

Complete the map. Then use it to write a story "fit for a king."

_____
_____
_____
_____
_____
_____
_____
_____

 Turn your story into a puppet show! Perform your puppet show for someone at home.

Name _____ Proofreading

The Father of Our Country

➡ *After you finish writing, go back and look for mistakes.*

Use the proofreading marks to correct eight mistakes in the letter.

mars = **Make a capital letter.**   ⟨?⟩ = **Add a question mark.**   ⟨!⟩ = **Add an exclamation point.**

⊙ = **Add a period.**   ⟨,⟩ = **Add a comma.**

Dear Friend,

my job as the first president of the United States was hard My friends and I had to make new laws new money, and new jobs. the capital was in New York when I became president. then it moved to Philadelphia. Is the capital still there. Who is the president today! I would love to see how the U.S. has changed over the past two hundred years?

Sincerely,

George Washington

On another piece of paper, write a letter to today's president. The White House address is: 1600 Pennsylvania Avenue Washington, D.C. 20500.

Name _____

Writing a friendly letter

Presidential Pen Pals

 A **friendly letter** has five parts: the date, greeting, body, closing, and signature.

Use the five parts to write a letter back to George Washington. Be sure to proofread your work for mistakes.

_____
(today's date)

_____,
(greeting)

(body)
_____
_____
_____
_____
_____
_____
_____
_____
_____

_____,
(closing)

_____
(your name)

Scholastic Success With Writing • Grade 2 47

Answer Key

Page 4
Many of; Our teacher; The reading; The globe; We study; Our class

Page 5
1. Art class; 2. Today we; 3. First, we; 4. The next; 5. My teacher; 6. Next week

Page 6
1. The blue whale is the largest animal in the world. 2. Even dinosaurs were not as large as the blue whale. 3. Blue whales are not part of the fish family. 4. The blue whale has no teeth. 5. Blue whales eat tiny sea creatures. 6. Blue whales have two blowholes.

Page 7
Sentences will vary.

Page 8
1. Where is the king's castle? 2. Who helped Humpty Dumpty? 3. Why did the cow jump over the moon? 4. Will the frog become a prince? 5. Could the three mice see?

Page 9
Sentences will vary.

Page 10
1. .; 2. ?; 3. ?; 4. .; 5. ?; 6. .; 7. ?; 8. .

Page 11
1. The sun is the closest star to Earth. 2. The sun is not the brightest star. 3. What is the temperature of the sun? 4. The sun is a ball of hot gas. 5. How large is the sun? 6. Will the sun ever burn out?

Page 12
Sentences will vary.

Page 13
Dear Mom and Dad,
   Camp is so cool! Today we went swimming. Do you know what the best part of camp is? I think fishing is my favorite thing to do. Did you feed my hamster? I really miss you.
Love, Dalton

Sentences will vary.

Page 14
1. .; 2. ?; 3. !; 4. ?; 5. .; 6. !; 7. ?; 8. .; 9. ?; 10. !; 11. .; 12. ?

Page 15
Sentences will vary.

Page 16
Sentences will vary.

Page 17
Sentences will vary.

Page 18
Sentences may vary. Possible answers: 1. A boy climbs a tree in his backyard. 2. A cat plays with fish in the living room. 3. A bunny eats a carrot in the garden.

Page 19
Sentences and pictures will vary.

Page 20
Lists of words will vary.

Page 21
Answers will vary. 1. fat, three; 2. wooden, cold; 3. Orange, sunny; 4. lazy, muddy; 5. thirsty, shallow; 6. funny, black

Page 22
Describing words will vary.

Page 23
Sentences will vary.

Page 24
Sentences will vary.

Page 25
Sentences will vary.

Page 26
1. The party was fun and exciting. 2. We blew up orange and red balloons. 3. We ate cake and ice cream. 4. The cake frosting was green and yellow. 5. We made a bookmark and a clay pot. 6. We brought games and prizes.

Page 27
1. These peanuts and pretzels are salty. 2. The first graders and second graders eat lunch at noon. 3. Where is the salt and pepper? 4. The napkins and forks are on the table. 5. Are the muffins and cookies in the oven? 6. Michael and Stephen bought lunch today.

Page 28
1. Fill a cup with water and add some flower seeds. 2. This will soften the seeds because they are hard. 3. Fill a cup with dirt while the seeds soak in water. 4. Bury the seeds in the cup until the dirt covers them. 5. Add water to the plant but do not add too much. 6. Set the cup in the sun so the plant will grow.

Page 29
Sentences will vary.

Page 30
Sentences will vary.

Page 31
Sentences will vary.

Page 32
Describing words will vary.
1. Sometimes I can see Mars, Jupiter, and Saturn with my telescope. 2. There are many stars in our galaxy. 3. Comets are large pieces of ice and rock. 4. The sun is really a huge star. 5. Is there life on any other planet? 6. Look at that beautiful shooting star! 7. Can you imagine traveling in space? 8. I think I saw a little alien.

Page 33
Describing words will vary.

Saturn is famous for the rings that surround it. Its rings are made of ice, rock, and dirt. The rings circle around the planet. Saturn is made of gas. Saturn's gases are lighter than water. That means Saturn would float if you put it into a tub of water. Saturn has a least 17 moons.

Page 34
1. took; 2. was; 3. saw; 4. many; 5. brought; 6. seen; 7. has; 8. are; 9. were; 10. saw; 11. wore; 12. going; 13. Does; 14. brought

Page 35
1. ~~brang~~, brought; 2. ~~seen~~, saw; 3. ~~gots~~, has; 4. ~~taked~~, took; 5. ~~is~~, are; 6. ~~runned~~, ran; 7. ~~got~~, have; 8. ~~was~~, were; 9. ~~saw~~, see; 10. ~~do~~, does; 11. ~~brang~~, brought; 12. ~~does~~, do

Page 36
Sentences will vary.

Page 37
Sentences will vary.

Page 38
Sentences will vary.

Page 39
Stories will vary.

Page 40
Sentences will vary.

Page 41
Sentences will vary.

Page 42
Sentences will vary.

Page 43
Answers will vary.

Page 44
Stories will vary.

Page 45
Stories will vary.

Page 46
Dear Friend,
   My job as the first president of the United States was hard. My friends and I had to make new laws, new money, and new jobs. The capital was in New York when I became president. Then it moved to Philadelphia. Is the capital still there? Who is the president today? I would love to see how the U.S. has changed over the past two hundred years!
Sincerely,
George Washington

Page 47
Letters will vary.